MEN COME
WITH
PRICE TAGS

TAMMY CALDERON

Copyright © 2018 Tammy Calderon
All rights reserved
First Edition

PAGE PUBLISHING, INC.
Conneaut Lake, PA

First originally published by Page Publishing 2018

ISBN 978-1-64298-022-6 (pbk)
ISBN 978-1-64298-023-3 (digital)

Printed in the United States of America

CONTENTS

Acknowledgments 5

Beautiful Woman 7

Preface 9

Introduction 11

1. Giving Too Much Too Soon 15

2. No Mo Build a Brotha, Too Far Down to be Helped Up 19

3. Put the Time in Up Front 24

4. Trust Your Instincts, God Is Speaking 29

5. Beware of the Church Boy 33

6. Don't get Caught in the Trick Bag 37

7. Just Because He Is a Good Man Does Not Make Him Husband Material 42

8. If It Don't Fit, Don't Force It 50

9. Beware of the Baller 55

10. Using Your Coochie to Supplement Your Income 58

11. The Facts Don't Lie.. 62

12. You Might Not Know Yourself as Well as You Think You Do.. 69

13. Stay in Your Own House 79

14. Beware of the Bad Boy.. 83

15. Pay Attention: Turn Down the Sound and Look at the Picture... 87

16. Mind Time 94

17. Investing Your Goodness and Getting Nothing in Return 98

18. I Will Take a Chance... 102

19. Doing What Seems Crazy 105

20. Good Girls, Beware... 109

21. Where Is Boaz... 119

ACKNOWLEDGMENTS

This book is dedicated to the good women and daughters who are dating in the twenty-first century. Those who still believe in traditional values. Those who are still believing God for a wonderful husband and healthy relationship.

To my mom, Hazel Porter, who helped shape me into the woman I am today. You are a strong and wonderful woman. Thank you for all your love and care down through the years.

To my bestie, Louis Bowman who has prayed and stayed with me through the best of times and the worst of times. Thanks for all of your support and friendship.

To all the friends who helped me to just get her done: Darrell Richard, Tamika Hicks, Tammy Porter, Dr. Jeff Dorsey and Kay Coney. Thank you for your countless hours of support and encouragement.

Special thanks to Felicia Permillion and Byron Bolton, your assistance was absolutely invaluable. Much, Much, Love to You!

All of you guys are the best, and I love you much!

BEAUTIFUL WOMAN

It is easy to be a pretty woman,
But to be a beautiful woman requires the
True distinction of strength and character,
Born from the trials and tribulations
One must go through in order to reach that
Sacred place which shapes not only the
Outside but the inside; therefore, beauty is not something that is merely physical.
A woman that is truly beautiful has a captivating presence, and whenever she walks into the room,
Everybody recognizes her confidence, her strength, and her beauty.

By Tammy Calderon

PREFACE

This book is written to women who are dating in the Modern World. The words of Pastor Devon Franklin captures the heart and soul of my message perfectly, and that is, "If you date well, you will marry well." As you read this book, imagine that you are sitting in your living room, with your favorite auntie or BFF, and you guys are having the most wonderful, heartfelt, conversation about men and relationships ever.

I hope that after reading this book, you will be inspired to make wiser choices in dating that will lead to relationships that are healthy, happy, and strong.

The purpose of this book is to cause you to *THINK!*

Think before you invest your time!

Think before you invest your emotions!

Think before you invest your heart!

Think before you make the decision about whom you will date, and ultimately, whom you will marry!

Let us stop going into our relationships mindlessly.

The emotional repercussions are costly. Can your heart afford it?

INTRODUCTION

What Price Will You Pay to Stay

Are we falling for men God never designed us to be with in the first place?

Have you ever said to yourself, "The next relationship that I enter into is going to be different, it is going to last, it is going to work," only to discover the results are the same? We have all been told that successful relationships take work, and this is very true. But why do you put in all the time, the prayer, the fasting, the endless giving, and giving, and giving, and forgiving? Doing everything that you know to do, everything that he told you he wanted you to do, and your relationship still did not last. It seemed as though God was silent and not listening to your prayers. Could it be that we are falling for men God never designed us to be with in the first place? God never designed us to be with men who are abusive, men who will not work and provide, men who are selfish and takers, men whose character is foul, nor men who are brazenly unfaithful and untrustworthy etc.

What price will you pay to stay? Certain men come with price tags. I'm talking about emotional price tags. And if you are not careful, you will spend an emotional fortune trying to connect with and stay with a man whom God never *designed* you to be with in the first place.

A lady came to me after observing my relationships and said, "Tam, your *picker* is broken."

"What in the world is a picker?" I asked.

And she said, "You don't have the ability **to pick/choose** a partner who is most suitable for you."

You know, I was getting with the guys who said they loved Jesus and went to church faithfully but did not have the lifestyle for Christ to back it up and whose personal lives were tow up from the flo' up. I was getting with the guys who had good jobs and a promising future, who dressed good, smelled good, and looked good, but their character was absolutely foul. You know the type that most young women dream of being with.

The point I'm making in this book is be smart, think deeply, and know yourself well enough so that you can choose wisely and avoid costly mistakes that can take years to recover from. I am asking you to calculate the cost, which means to honestly evaluate your relationship or potential relationship; and consider how the consequences (both positive and negative) of that relationship will affect your life, your children's life, and the lives of those around you who love you. Choose wisely from the start so that you're not jumping from man to man to man; your heart will not be able to sustain all the hits.

Let's fine-tune our "pickers" and increase the probability of building relationships that will be successful and go the distance even through the toughest of times. I am not trying to tell you what to do, but I am trying to get you to think before you do it.

I felt compelled to write this book because so many of us go into relationships blindly, ignorant of what it is that we are really up against. I hope this book opens eyes and helps us to avoid costly mistakes. And above all, I hope it helps us to make wise choices so that we can have happy, healthy, and long lasting relationships.

My prayer for every woman reading this book is that God will bless you with a man who is most suitable for you and that He will bless you with that man who will be good to you and give you the love that you *soooo* awesomely deserve. Amen.

CHAPTER ONE

Giving Too Much Too Soon

He must earn the right to obtain special benefits and privileges.

We are exhilarated surprising him, cooking for him, and serving him. You want to let him know that beyond the shadow of a doubt you are with him all the way. You give and give and give. One of the biggest mistakes a girl can make in a relationship is to give too much too soon. Mister has not even asked you to be exclusive yet, however, you have forsaken all, and made him your one and only without him earning that place.

We take on the wifey role far too soon. We take on the wifey role before the relationship gets a chance to bond, settle, and gel. In other words, have you emotionally captivated him to the point where it is you that he can't wait to run to and give to? Yes, a man loves to give to the woman that he loves.

Aren't you supposed to give your all? No! Not until your relationship reaches a certain level. Before that level, you are setting yourself up to be taken advantage of. You are setting yourself up to be taken for granted and handled carelessly because you have made things far *too* easy for him. Remember, a man is a hunter by nature, and he will eventually disrespect that which he has not paid a price for. I am in no way telling you to play ridiculously hard to get. All I'm saying is, don't give yourself away too easily.

Signs that show you may be giving too much too soon:

- You're the one doing most or all of the giving.
- You're the one doing most of the calling and texting.
- By the first or third date, you are an open book. You have told him all about how you've been mistreated. Dude is not your friend, no need to divulge ammo that may be used against you later.
- You've known him three months or less and you're already purchasing big ticket items for him. Buying all his kids school clothes. Paying for you to go on vacations etc.
- After two months of knowing him you have already loaned him a large sum of money.
- After one month, he already has the keys to your house and you hardly know him.
- You make all the plans, pay most of the time, and buy all the gifts. He forgets to even buy you a card.
- Before the man makes any type of commitment, you pour yourself into helping him; even to the point of ignoring your own life and the needs of your children.
- You are w-a-a-a-a-a-a-y too available for him any time he wants, even at your inconvenience.
- You are always doing something for him, there is no reciprocity; all the while he does very little for you.

> He's beginning to pull away, and you keep doing more and more to get him to stay: only to find, that he's engaged to home girl down the street who he said treated him like crap.

Does he appreciate all your giving? No, he does not. This is because a man wants a woman who values herself. If you give yourself away too easily, he knows subconsciously that the value you place on yourself is not that high. And, if you don't place value upon yourself, then he certainly won't either. Men will value and respect you in accordance to the value and respect that you place upon yourself. Take your time, and allow him to earn that most precious part of you, your heart.

$ CALCULATE THE COST $

What may be the cost of giving too much too soon?

- He may not choose you. After you have given everything, he still may not choose you.
- He will continuously take from you; laugh and talk about what a fool you are with his friends.
- You will lose sight of your own feelings and needs; making sacrifices at your own expense and at the expense of your children.
- You will give him everything and he still won't love you.
- If the relationship continues, are you setting yourself up to become an enabler? Givers attract takers. If your man is irresponsible, does your giving make him even more irresponsible? You will spend an emotional fortune trying to connect with and stay with this man.

A SELAH MOMENT:

Are you taking on the wifey role far too soon? If you are in a relationship, is he treating you like a woman that he values highly? If not, what are you going to do about it?

_____

_____

_____

CHAPTER TWO

No Mo Build a Brotha, Too Far Down to be Helped Up

Do not invest money, time, or energy in a man who is not actively pursuing his goals because he is only pitching fantasy to you and himself.

We've all been told, read about, or heard about women who helped a man while he was down and the relationship turned out beautifully. But I say to you, sometimes a man may be too far down for you to help him up. We hear how Michelle Obama raised up Prez and helped him become the most powerful man in the world. Well President Obama graduated from Harvard Law School and was a lawyer to begin with. Success was evident for him. Don't you think he was already headed for a high measure of success with or without Michelle?

The man that you help up must already be headed in the direction of success. If you decide that you want to help a man out, make sure he has some type of history of success: meaning that you see him passionately working toward his vision, goals, and dreams. Does he at least have a high school diploma/GED, has he finished college or is he going to college, or has he worked on his job for a long time. He has to be doing something! The key word here is **doing,** not talking about it but being about it.

However, us girls have been led to believe if we see a brother down, help him out, help him get on his feet. I say to you, there are certain situations that we should avoid and not waste our time or energy on all together. If a man is not actively, passionately, pursuing his goals and you see little to no evidence or progress: Do not invest money, time, or energy because he is only pitching fantasy to you and himself, this brother is not ready to be helped up.

The following are signs that may signal that a man may just be a talker and not a doer:

- ➢ He is constantly pursuing some multi-level marketing scheme, and has never made any progress. He has more money going out of the house than what he has coming in. He's been doing this same kind of "business" for years, and refuses to see that it is not working and that he needs to focus his energies into something that will yield consistent income. This brother is not ready to be helped up.
- ➢ He cannot keep a job and is always complaining about and has difficulty working with his boss and co-workers. He does not realize that he is the problem, no matter how many times you or his friends have informed him, that he is the one who needs to make the adjustment. He is constantly moving from job to job and shows no signs of stability. This brother is not ready to be helped up.
- ➢ Bruh, bruh has been working at the same dead end job for years. He works on commission, sometimes he gets

paid and sometimes he doesn't. He passionately tells you about the business that he is getting ready to start. He's been telling the same vision for the last ten years and has not hit a lick at a snake. He has done absolutely nothing toward making his dream happen. You ask him what he is doing to make it happen and he gets turned off, sad, and mad. Girlfriend, this brother is not ready to be helped up.

- He has convinced you to support him financially while he pursues his dreams. When you come home from work, he is playing video games, sleeping, or gone. You ask him how the project is going, he blows up and gets mad and tells you he's been making calls all day or has been in the studio; when in actuality, he has only made one phone call and hasn't been anywhere. This man is lazy and trifling. Girlfriend, this brother is not ready to be helped up.
- He went to prison when he was a teenager, now in his late twenties/thirties he is getting out, but has done nothing to develop himself those years he's been in the slammer. Girlfriend, this brother is not ready to be helped up.
- He has never paid his own bills, lived in his own place, or been responsible for himself. This brother is not ready to be helped up.
- He cannot read or write or do basic math. I don't care how good he looks, kiss, or smell. I don't care if he looks like success itself. Girlfriend, fo' sho', this brother is too far down to be helped up.

Time is valuable, so don't waste it on someone who is not worthy of the investment!

$ CALCULATE THE COST $

What may be the cost of helping a man that is too far down?

- He will eventually pull you down along with him.
- Your credit will be damaged and you may go bankrupt trying to finance his dreams; now your credit score is too low to finance the home and things that you've always wanted.
- You will be empty and have nothing to give to anyone else, not even to yourself and your children. Raising him up will deplete all of your strength and wear you plumb out.
- If his dreams do not go according to his plan, he will blame you for his failure because he believes that you did not contribute enough help, even though you gave all you had.
- You will lose sight of, and miss opportunities, to create your own dreams and goals sacrificing to help him out. If it were not for him, you could have been further down the road. Now you are behind where you should be and have to make up for lost time.

A SELAH MOMENT:

Is the man you are with too far down to be helped up? Why or Why not? Is he consistently pursuing his goals and you see proof and progress?

_____

_____

_____

CHAPTER THREE

Put the Time in Up Front

How can you develop intimacy or get to know a man's heart if you cannot talk to him?

Relationships that are happy and healthy just don't happen automatically, both people must be dedicated to creating something that is wonderful and special. Most people wait until they are married before they start putting serious work into their relationship, only to find, that their situation is unbearable and cannot be worked out. I'm suggesting that you put the work in upfront while dating; if your goal is to be in a happy, healthy, and lasting relationship. **Find out all the truth you possibly can before you marry this man.** You **must explore** the deep core areas that will make or break your relationship such as how you handle conflict, can you love him the way he is if those things you want him to change never change. Can you talk to / communicate with him easily? Is he a soft place to fall when you are at your most vulnerable point? Is he an impulsive decision-maker? Does he mindlessly spend every dime he earns?

Can you be partners, moving in the same direction? Do you want the same lifestyle? Do you have the same goals for how you will live your life? What are his habits? Is he a gambler? Does he suffer from some type of psychosis or mental disorder? Is he easily angered? How will you raise and discipline your children, etc.?

Observe, observe, observe! Nine times out of ten, when you ask your man the above questions, he is either going to tell you what he thinks you want to hear or what he believes to be true about himself. However, in reality, it may or may not be true. My father always told me, turn down the sound and look at the picture. There should be congruency which means that a person's actions and words should be the same. If the actions and the words do not line up, hold up, this may not be the most suitable partner for you. Don't be afraid to walk away for fear this may be the best there is. There are always more fish in the sea.

You have to be able to talk about and work through serious issues that plague or may plague your relationship. Seriously think about this. If you are dating a man and you are at the point of talking in depth about things; and he doesn't want to or is very uncomfortable doing so, I would question his level of commitment to having a lasting relationship with you. When a man **is ready** and wants a woman, he is more than willing to answer important questions concerning life, goals, children, or whatever. For the most part, men do not like to talk deeply about important issues, therefore, you will have to be prayerful and strategic. You will have to bring up the subject matter at the right time and in the right way.

You **HAVE TO** be able to talk, to communicate. If your communication does not flow freely, your bonding and your intimacy will be effected. Communication that is satisfying bonds hearts together. Talking helps you to get to know and understand one another. How can you develop intimacy or get to know a man's heart if you cannot talk to him? Every serious relationship that I have ever been in or seen, the man who was serious about me, did not mind answering the "deep" questions. He may not have ever thought about those questions before or knew the answer, however, he was willing to think about them and get back to me with some discussion. Men on the other hand, who were talking commitment but were not serious; either made excuses, gave shallow answers, or just avoided the questions all together.

Richard Marcinko said, "The more you sweat in training, the less you'll bleed in the war." In other words, put in the work on the front end, so that you won't have to go through a lot of drama on the back end. The institution of the family is at stake, we cannot afford to take the decision of who we will spend the rest of our lives with lightly. Be wise, the future of our children and our community is depending on it.

$ CALCULATE THE COST $

What may be the costs of not putting the time in up front?

 Your relationship will not flourish and be the best it can possibly be if you can not communicate and work together. If you do not put the time in, then your relationship will not thrive. Nothing that is neglected thrives.

 If you are not on the same page, you will experience much drama and fight more than you should. Drama breeds stress. Stress breeds illnesses. A stressful relationship will affect your health.

- An unhealthy environment will damage your children. The decisions that you make will affect your children.

- If you marry him, you may have a toleration marriage. A toleration marriage is one in which both partners are unhappy, but will stay in the relationship because they feel they cannot leave. The reasons given are usually due to material wealth accumulated, the children, or not being able to live on their own and afford a quality lifestyle.

- If the two of you do not put in the proper effort, even though the relationship started off great, the relationship will eventually die on the vine, meaning it will just fizzle out.

- Divorce! Divorce is costly, especially for the children. Take your time and do it right the first time.

- Wasted Time! As a young woman, you will not understand the concept of wasted time until later on. You will sit and think about all the time you wasted with men who did not even deserve you.

A SELAH MOMENT:

Are you and your partner together creating a relationship that is wonderful and satisfying? OR Are you the only one putting in all the work and carrying the relationship? If so, what needs to happen?

_____

_____

_____

CHAPTER FOUR

Trust Your Instincts, God Is Speaking

Instincts are God's Warning signs. Oblivion is costly!

You may call it a sixth sense, an unction, a knowing, or a gut feeling. We may have assigned many names to this sense, but it is actually God who is speaking. This instinct is an innate guide, and when God speaks, He does not lie. I could have avoided a lot of heartache, pain, and wasted time had I listened to my instinct. God gave us this sixth sense to guide, warn, and protect us.

When you have no peace about a relationship, stop and listen, God is speaking. When things are going great but you sense that something is not quite right. Stop and listen! God is speaking! This is your red flag and sign that something is wrong. However, we go ahead anyways because we have no evidence to substantiate how we are feeling. After all, we are having a wonderful time in the relationship. If you get a funny feeling or an uneasy feeling about a dude in your gut, pump your brakes and proceed with caution, God is speaking. Experience has taught me not to question this feeling but to put an end to whatever relationship I'm in immediately. Every time I have had no peace and felt uneasy about a person, the relationship ended disastrously. The voice of God has been 100 percent right.

Sometimes a man can hide who he is so well that you will never see it coming. The only source that one can have to identify this deceiver is the Holy Spirit. Pray for discernment because deception is becoming the name of the game. The dating game is becoming ruthless. The deceiver will say and do all the right things, be extremely good to you and your children. Oh my God, you think he is heaven sent. He will go to church with you. He will ask to marry you and set the date. He will bring you before friends and family as his fiancée. He will spend time with you, call you all the time, make you feel like you are number one.

However, this man's main goal is to get you to drop your guard and trust him completely so that he can control you. He knows that once he has your heart, he has your mind. And once he has your heart and mind, he knows that he has all of you: and he can manipulate you as he pleases. Lately, I have read and heard men say that it is no longer good enough to just have a woman's body, they want her soul; her heart and her mind.

I was shocked that they admitted something like this and asked, "Why?" I was told that when you get a woman's heart, she can't go anywhere. You can do anything you want including see other women and she will still be down for you. I could not believe what I was hearing. I should not have been surprised because a few years back, we were bouncing to the tunes that told men it was cool to be a pimp and a playa. We laughed and thought it was cute and harmless, however the spirit of that message took root. Music/the media is a very powerful tool of influence. Please do not underestimate its power in shaping our core values and belief systems. We have seen a whole value system wiped out because of it. Hell has a strategy! The enemy is very, very, clever and uses tactics that can go undetected and are seemingly harmless, but ever so lethal.

Slow down! Look deeply! Listen! There is no more time to waste, oblivion is costly.

$ CALCULATE THE COST $

What may be the costs of ignoring your instincts?

Ignoring your instincts could cause you to:

- Connect with someone who is a toxic person. Negativity is contagious and will eventually bring you down.
- Connect with someone who will cause you to be in a dangerous situation. If you stay, you will actually lose your life or go to jail.
- Connect with someone who could take you away from your core values and beliefs.
- Connect with someone who will drain you financially and cause you to hit rock bottom. It will be next to impossible to recover from the setback, especially at your age.
- Cause you to connect with someone who could take your focus away from God and cause you to stray from His path.

A SELAH MOMENT:

What are you sensing in your spirit that God is saying about your relationship? If you are not in a relationship, what is He saying about the guy you want to have a relationship with?

_____

_____

_____

CHAPTER FIVE

Beware of the Church Boy

Don't let the position, gifting or anointing fool you!

There is nothing more appealing or satisfying than being with a man who truly loves and has a relationship with Almighty God. A man who will grab your hands and pray over you and your children; one who knows how to protect, to provide for, and take care of his household. And, there is nothing more disappointing and emotionally shattering than to be with a Pretender, a wolf in sheep's clothing.

The church boy is the most cunning of all players and knows how to tear the walls of a good woman down. Who are they? They are your priest, your pastors, your bishops, your deacons, Sunday school teachers, choir directors, praise and worship leaders etc.

There are two categories that the Church Boy falls into: The Real Man of God (the RMG-who is the Christian boy) or the Fake Man of God (the FMG). Initially the church boy and the

Christian boy look the same. What is the difference between the two? The real man of God is the one who truly loves God and tries to live according to His word: though he fall, he will repent, get back up and strive to do better. He is a good husband and father to his children etc. If you marry a true man of God, you have done well. Of course, he is not perfect and has his faults, but nothing that is earth shattering or a deal breaker.

On the other hand, The fake man of God is a church going man, he loves going to God's house. He speaks the Christian language, everyone speaks well of him, he can quote scriptures and may perform various charitable deeds too. He seems like a great guy! Most FMG's are highly gifted and anointed in the area that God has called them to work in. He will grab your hands and pray with you and lead you before the throne of grace. His car is usually filled with Christian music and sermons. He will tell you how he has not had sex in a long time and how he wants to wait, because he is now doing things differently. Everything about him will seem legitimate, but it isn't. Time and observing his character will reveal who he is.

A few characteristics to help you distinguish the difference between the RMG and the FMG:

The Real Man of God

1. He will have a moral compass. He's not taken back when you say you are saving yourself for marriage and don't want to sleep with him before that time. He understands that, and God help his po lil weak soul, he will try to practice that too. Girls, we really need to intercede for our men in this area.

2. He will have a real relationship with Christ. His beliefs and values will line up with the Word of God. There is evidence in his character and his actions that he has a relationship with Christ.
3. He will treat you with respect, dignity, and honor.
4. He's not playing games.
5. He will work at being a good boyfriend or husband and father.
6. You will have a peace about being with him.
7. He will love you the right way. His love will be true and genuine.

The Fake Man of God

1. You will have no peace in being with him; although everything is going great, something in your spirit will be unsettled.
2. He is a Masterful Deceiver. He gets you to trust him completely, then he turns on you. Once he knows that you are hooked, this is when his true colors will begin to show.
3. He will fake morality. He will pretend that he doesn't want sex, he can wait. All the while, doing and saying things that will cause you to fall. And, of course he will be having sex with someone else all the while pretending to be waiting.
4. He has charisma but no character. He can preach, teach, or sing the whole church happy. His spiritual gifts are awesome, but his personal life is tow up from the floor up.
5. He is a Masterful Manipulator. You know he is lying and you have proof, but somehow you end up believing what he said. He can speak and act with such con-

viction that you will begin to believe him over what you know is true. He will make you doubt yourself and question your own sanity.
6. He may be engaged to 2 or 3 women at the same time.
7. He will become a taker. He only gives in order to receive. He will quit working and say that God has called him into the ministry full time and ask you to fund the ministry. OR, he will ask you to continuously fund "church projects" all the while taking the money for his own personal gain.
8. He might be on the down low.

The Good Book says it like this, "You will know them by their fruit," Mathew 7:15-20. Time always reveals the true character of a person. Therefore, slow down and take your time, so that you can see who a man truly is before making any type of big investment.

Mike Murdock says, "Patience is the weapon that forces deceit to reveal itself." A man's actions and character will always identify who he truly is. Continue praying and asking God for discernment.

CHAPTER SIX

Don't get Caught in the Trick Bag

Sometimes feelings will lie to you and tell you that you are strong when you are actually weak.

Many women have started out with the mindset of I'm just gonna play around with this little tenderoni who is 15-20 years younger than I. OR I'm just gonna play around with this married man, get what I want, then move on. OR I'm just in it to get what I need, only to find themselves caught in the trick bag. You might ask, "What is the trick bag?" The trick bag is that place called before you know it, you done messed around and fell in love, and you never intended to do that. You lied to yourself and told yourself that you only wanted to have a little fun and get your bills paid. You lied to and convinced yourself that you did not want to be in a committed relationship, this was just something to do.

Sometimes a man can be so loving and kind that it will cause you to drop all defenses and your rationale for being with him. We all underestimate that thing called loving kindness. When a man is good to you, it will melt you down like butter. Now you are trapped in a relationship that you know you have no business being in a'tal. You want to leave but can't because you have developed deep feelings for him; and you never intended to do that. If the truth be told, from the very start, your inner most longing was to be with someone who would love you right; it was never about the money or just playing around. Baby girl, you must always examine your feelings carefully because sometimes feelings will lie to you and mislead you; causing you to think that you are strong when you are actually weak. Just because you feel something deeply, doesn't mean you should continue doing it. In order to move on, pray and ask God to remove all feelings and soul ties that you have developed for Mister Wrong.

Shakespeare said "to thine own self be true." Meaning you can lie to everybody else, but baby girl please don't lie to yourself. It's a dangerous thing when you have not spent enough time with yourself, to know yourself truthfully. You should always know and admit to yourself when your "love tank" is empty. You should always know and admit to yourself when you are lonely. You should always know and admit to yourself when you are desperate. It is these times of deprivation that will cause you to get involved in a situation that is not good for you. But because you underestimated your need for love, you deceived yourself into thinking it's cool, I can handle it, I'm just doing this until something better comes along. He's just my transitional lover and before you know it, you done got yourself placed in the trick bag.

My advice is, don't start what you do not intend to finish. **Your emotions cannot sustain the wear and tear; this is how dysfunction begins**. Always keep your main goal in mind, and that is to have a long, lasting, healthy, and wonderful relationship. Matters of the heart are tricky. Don't allow your temporary need to deceive you and drive you into making decisions that you will regret and ultimately pay a high price for later on. Girlfriend, your value is far above rubies, there is no need to settle.

$ CALCULATE THE COST $

What may be the cost of being caught in the trick bag?

- You could end up with someone that you truly do not want to be with. He is good for your right now but not your future.
- You feel helpless and out of control because you have become so dependent on this person.
- You are a young woman, and you are dating a man 20 plus years older than you. Please consider the following:
  - You didn't plan to stay, however, you are still there because he is so good to you financially. As you grow and mature into a woman, you will realize that you want and need more than just getting your bills paid.
  - Depending on how old and controlling the old coot really is: you could end up having no voice and no rights. He calls all the shots and makes all the decisions.
  - You are now in your 40's, at the peak of your sexuality, and you are still with him. Men when they get older, also go through the change of life- male menopause. Their menopause affects them sexually and psychologically, just like it does us. Hopefully, he will be able to take Viagra to assist

> him with his erectile dysfunction. If Viagra cannot help him, a man normally shuts down and will not even try to engage in any sexual activity. It is next to impossible to remain faithful to a man who will not even try to satisfy you sexually.
> You could end up being his care taker; and you are still young, vivacious, and beautiful, having to walk around with a man who looks like your grandfather.
> You might think, "Well, I'll just divorce him." Honey, the quality of man is changing seemingly every 5 years. If you think finding a man that is husband material is hard now, in the next 10-20 years, you will need a miracle in order to find a quality man. Yes, even with old school dudes; most of them have bought into the media hype and want a girl who is as close to looking like a model as they can find. It is best to get it right the first time.

- Feeling that you are stuck in a relationship can turn you into an angry and bitter person.
- Wasted Time. You will never be able to recover all the time and tears invested into the wrong relationship.

A SELAH MOMENT:

Be honest with yourself and evaluate what your future will look like with this man. Will you really be happy with him?

_____

_____

_____

CHAPTER SEVEN

Just Because He Is a Good Man Does Not Make Him Husband Material

A man who is husband material must at least have the basics in place, which are sufficient income, good character, and proven love for you.

If your goal in dating is to get married, then date men who are husband material. Just because he is a good man does not make him husband material. You might ask, "What is the difference between a good man and one who is husband material? Initially, the two men look the same, for they share similar characteristics. I will discuss the qualities of the good man first, then contrast the difference between the two later in this chapter. A good man is one who is nice and respectful. He is there for you, loves, and supports you. You seemingly can depend on him. He even loves Jesus and attends church faithfully and will do anything that you ask him to do. However, there are some major issues that he has that will sooner or later become the focal point and downfall of your relationship. Below I have provided examples of common issues signifying that your man may be a good man but not husband material.

Some major issues to consider before giving Mr. Good Man the time of day:

- **A man who is in prison or just getting out of prison is not husband material.** I KNOW, I KNOW, I KNOW, he says he's gonna go to church, work, and do what's right by you and the kids. But as soon as he gets home, he starts running the streets and hanging out with his homeboys and other women. Honey, GIVE THE MAN TIME TO BE PROVEN. He needs to prove that he is who he says he is. Give the man time to get to know himself. At least let him get a job and work for about a year to see if he will sustain employment and not quit or get fired after a few weeks or months. Most of the time, they do something crazy and end up back in jail anyways. Baby girl, I know you want to be married. Take your time! You may be saving yourself from a lot of heartache and pain. And whatever you do, don't get pregnant because if he goes back to jail, you got another load you have to pull all by yourself.

- **If a man's character is foul,** he is not husband material. I know, he is the man of your dreams. He is successful, a man of God, handsome, and really in to you. However, even though he is a "good man," he is not husband material. You are focused on his potential and the man that he could become. The man that you have created in your head does **not yet** exist. This man is ultimately very selfish and immature. He does not have the character or the maturity to treat you like you deserve to be treated.

- **He does not care about how he talks to you, he has no filters.** He is very condescending, belittling, and talks down to you making you feel worthless. He hurts your feelings to the core, especially in front of company. Whatever you do for him is never good enough; he always finds faults.

- **He has no job; nothing or very little to bring to the table**. You are already at a major disadvantage before you even start. He will become a burden. He is not husband material because a woman will NEVER respect a man who does not provide. I don't care how hard she tries. Sooner or later you are going to get tired of pulling the entire load. You are going to want more and will eventually end up resenting him. God never designed you to carry the whole load. A man needs respect in order to thrive and feel good about himself. A decent man will never respect himself if he cannot provide. And besides that, financial hardship is one of the major causes of divorce. Why go into a relationship/marriage with a major deficit? The relationship has failed before it even got started.
- **He is a great guy and you love him; however, he will not COMMIT**. This man is not husband material. You knew he would not commit when you hooked up with him. HE IS NOT READY FOR MARRIAGE! He has been telling you and showing you, but you're still buggin' and asking God if he is the one. You've been with him well over two years now. Stop praying, asking, and believing God to move on his heart and yada, yada, yada. God does not have to speak to you because the man himself has already given you the answer. He has told you repeatedly that he does not want to marry. Believe you me, a man knows after about three months or less, whether he is going to marry you or not. If a man will not commit to you

after more than two years, something of vital importance is missing from your relationship. Something is terribly wrong. In a situation like this, I have a simple formula that I use to determine if a man is the one. The formula goes like this, the man is the one because he says he is the one. The man is the one because you say he is the one. The man is the one because God agrees that he is the one. If anyone in that formula is not in agreement, then he is not the one. It's just that simple.

- **A man who you know has an addiction or is a newly recovering addict** is not husband material. You will spend an **EMOTIONAL FORTUNE** trying to keep him from relapsing and spending all the family's bill money. I've seen many times where women pop in and scoop these men up far too soon because they get a snap shot of the potential product that God is so skillfully and wonderfully putting together. Get out of the way, God's work is not finished. God's work will either be delayed or not completed because you are all up in the mix before the time. As a matter of fact, recovering addicts are not even supposed to date until they have a certain length of time in sobriety.

- **Is he done with the streets?** If not, this man is not husband material. Baby girl you don't have to share. Sharing does not work anyways because somebody is always going to come up short. When a man is juggling women; his attention, resources, money, and love is divided and he cannot give you what you need. Something will always be missing. Your mind will never be able to rest when he is not with you. You will always have that gnawing, sick feeling of pain in the center of your gut telling you that something is wrong.

If he is ready for marriage, he will be true to you and you alone.

- **Is he violent toward you or others in any way form or fashion verbally or physically?** If so, this man is not husband material. If he is violent to others and not to you, believe me, your day is coming. If he is beating you while dating, he will beat you more if you marry him. Does he say things to belittle you and cause you to feel bad about yourself? Believe me, if you stay, you will have no self-esteem left at all.
- **For the Christian woman, is he a believer?** If not, he is not husband material. The word of God tells us in II Corinthians 6:14, that we should not be unequally yoked together with an unbeliever. Take time to get to know whether or not he is a **true believer** or just a church goer. This will make all the difference in the world in your relationship if you decide to marry. Pray for discernment and ask God to reveal who he truly is.

Now that we know more about Mr. Goodman, let's look at a man who is husband material. A man who is husband material must at least have **the basics in place**. He should have steady income/employment. He does not need you or his family to supplement his income in order to make ends meet. He should have his own ride, phone, and place to live. He is independent, all his needs are met adequately.

- He has good character and shows that he is responsible. He is a man of his word. He has your back and you can depend on him.
- He is done chasing women and is ready to commit. He makes you feel **secure** in the relationship, you know that he loves you and that you are number one.

- ➤ He takes care of his children.
- ➤ He has no or is not overcoming any vices such as drugs and alcohol. If he is, he has enough years of sobriety to prove that he takes full responsibility for his own well-being. You do not have to remind, encourage, or force him to maintain his sobriety.
- ➤ He is not verbally abusive or violent.
- ➤ And, above all, he does all those things that make you feel loved, respected, and supported. This man is husband material.

As you can see, the good man and the man who is husband material share some of the same qualities. The major difference between the two is that the good man is not in position to husband a wife.

I have now stopped asking God to send me a good man, I am now asking God to send me a man who is husband material.

I hope I have provided insight as to why we should not even consider dating a man who is not husband material. It is a waste of time, if your goal is marriage! Be patient! Wait! Choose wisely initially!

$ CALCULATE THE COST $

What may be the cost of dating a good man who is not husband material?

 You will lower your standard and settle.

 You will be in for one exhaustive battle trying to turn the good man into husband material.

- Marital dissatisfaction. If you marry him, those unresolved issues will lead to separation or divorce.
- Wasted time. Do not take time for granted; in the long run, time will cost you much more than you think.
- Unable to have children. You once wanted children, but are now too old to have them because you continued dating the wrong type of man or you stayed in a bad relationship far too long.

A SELAH MOMENT:

If you want to be married, is the man you are dating husband material? Why or Why not?

_____

_____

_____

CHAPTER EIGHT

If It Don't Fit, Don't Force It

Loving is not supposed to be one continuous hard struggle.

Both of you really want the relationship to work, but for whatever reason it doesn't. He is husband material and you will make a wonderful wife. But being with him is like trying to put a square peg into a round hole. You are trying *so* hard to make it work. But it just doesn't. It is true that relationships require hard work, but not to this degree. You leave his presence feeling drained and frustrated. Loving is not supposed to be that hard. Loving is not supposed to be one continuous arduous struggle. You feel that if you leave him, you will be making a terrible mistake because good men who are husband material are hard to come by, so you better make it work. Let it go, he is not the most suitable partner for you.

Signs that may indicate he is not the most suitable partner for you:

- There is absolutely no chemistry and very little attraction on your part. You stay because he treats you well; however, you do not treat him well. You cringe on the inside when he touches you. You find yourself snapping at him and being mean to him for no reason at all. Baby girl, let him go! This man, is not the most suitable man for you.

- You misunderstand each other a lot. For whatever reason, he always misses the true meaning of what you are saying and vice versa. When you are in tune with one another, communication flows smooth and easy.

- You push each other's button without even trying to. Instead of bringing out the best in each other, you bring out the worst.

- He has a few values, beliefs, or habits that really make you uncomfortable. How can two walk together unless they agree?

- You have a different life flow. For example, he likes to blast his music first thing in the morning and play it sort of loud all day long. However, you like a quite and tranquil atmosphere where you can meditate and think.

- You love to be affectionate. He doesn't like it so much. He is constantly pushing you away and you are constantly feeling rejected.

➤ He is a short man and you really, really, really like tall men. He is the best man that you have ever had. You are trying with everything within you to love him, but you just don't. You think to yourself how selfish and immature, I will grow to love him. Let it go, you will only damage a good man. You cannot force yourself to be mature before the time.

➤ You are a go-getter, he is comfortable working on what you consider to be a dead-end job. He wants nothing more out of life than what he already has. He is truly happy where he is, however, everything about this dude is great, it is only this one thing that bothers you to the bone. You cannot get past it. Let it go. If you stay, you may be in for one exhaustive battle.

➤ He enjoys doing things spontaneously the majority of the time; whereas you like to plan things out. This bothers you to the bone and you can not seem to make any adjustments to make it work out for you.

➤ You are bored to smithereens with him, but you still force yourself to stay because you feel that boredom is too shallow of a reason to leave.

God has more fish in the sea that are more suitable and right for you. Loving should flow and be harmonious. Be patient but proactive! The right man will come.

$ CALCULATE THE COST $

What may be the cost of forcing something that is not there?

- The relationship will be vulnerable to outside influences. You both will seek to fill the void. Whatever is missing from the relationship, you will eventually seek to get it from someone or somewhere else.

- You will scar and damage a perfectly good man. You will turn a good man bad because of your poor treatment of him and selfishness of not setting him free to be loved truly.

- "You can't make your heart feel something it won't," says the song writer. If you marry him, your relationship will become a toleration marriage. 'Til death do us part is a long time to endure someone who irritates you to the core.

- The relationship will never work out no matter how hard you try.

- You will not be fulfilled or satisfied if you continue in the relationship with him.

A SELAH MOMENT:

Are you trying too hard to make something happen that isn't there? Does he fulfill you?

_____

_____

_____

CHAPTER NINE

Beware of the Baller

OMG! You are absolutely elated! He chose you above all the rest! You know that he is going to treat you like a goddess, and will spare no expense taking you out on the town. He looks good, smells good, and is groomed to the nine. He demands and commands respect. He has swagger and is confident, and all the way on top of his game. He is highly financially successful and secure, and will make an excellent provider.

Women love the title of being the girlfriend of or wife of a highly successful man. Let's face it, being taken care of feels really good. The men who fall into this category are your professional athletes, businessmen, politicians, doctors, lawyers, rappers, musicians, actors, rockstars, etc. Women seem to just lose it over this type of man. Although the perks are outstanding, being with this type of man is not all that it's cracked up to be.

$ CALCULATE THE COST $

What may be the cost of dating the baller?

- They love their work! And, work is extremely time consuming. Their livelihood has priority above everything else, including wife and kids.

- Just because he makes a good living does not mean he will also make a good husband.

- This type of man is usually very superficial and narcissistic; it's all about him. He has no depth of character. Because a man of means can have just about anything he desires, he does not have to take time to develop his character. You will need more than money in order to have a happy and fulfilling relationship. Most women who marry these types of men are normally unfulfilled in the areas of bonding and emotional intimacy.

- Marrying this type of man almost always ends in divorce. Most women are ill prepared to take on the demands of being married to a man in the big leagues.

- He is addicted to variety, therefore, your shelf life more than likely will be short. One woman does not hold his interest very long. Whether you marry or date him, cheating is common with this type of man and is an acceptable practice in his world. He will continuously attract women who will throw themselves at him, get used to it.

- Prepare to be alone most of the time. He is hardly ever home, and if you marry him, you will be raising the kids all by yourself.

MEN COME WITH PRICE TAGS

- In dating, he may do a Hoodini on you. Mr. Man will ghost you, meaning he will just disappear for no reason. One minute you're with him and everything is great, and the next minute he stops coming over and calling. All of a sudden, he's really busy at work, and have a million excuses as to why he cannot see you. The truth of the matter is, he's moved on.

- In dating this type of man, he is usually vague and unpredictable. He will not want you to pin him down on anything. Good luck if you can get a straight answer from him, if he answers you at all.

- If you do marry him, you may have to wear a condom and practice safe sex. You're never quite sure of what little surprise he might bring home.

- His work will impact just about every area of your life from something as simple as having dinner uninterrupted. Being in the lime light will soon get old and can become a major nuisance.

CHAPTER TEN

Using Your Coochie to Supplement Your Income

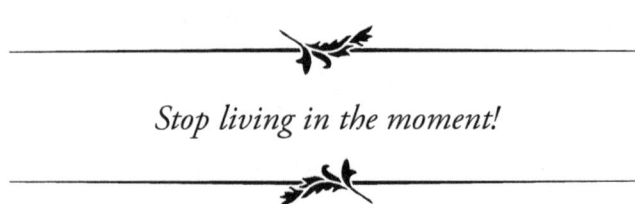

Stop living in the moment!

Have you prepared adequately for your future? Stop depending on his money to live and make ends meet. Stop living to buy the next Prada purse or Jimmy Choo shoes or whatever expensive thing that gives you bragging rights. You never want to put yourself in a position where you **have to** depend on another person's money to live a quality life.

Let me explain why I used the word supplement and income. Supplemental income is usually a term associated with governmental programs designed to pay benefits to people who have limited income and resources. This term applies to many women in this aspect: If old boy don't kick in, you can't pay your house note or rent, you can't pay your phone bill, you and your kids can't eat. You cannot maintain the lifestyle that you have become accustomed to living without his money supplementing your income.

Perhaps you are accustomed to making your own money, however you're involved in a relationship that you know you should not be in, but can't break away from because you are used to the extra money and perks that old boy is kicking down.

I am not saying that you are not supposed to receive money and gifts from your man. What I AM SAYING is whether his money is there or not, you can still live the quality of life that you want or have become accustomed to. I am saying, don't let getting money/extra money be your reason for staying with a man who treats you poorly. Many women work on jobs that cannot sustain their lifestyle. However, rather than go and get more education or training in order to take care of themselves sufficiently, they look for a man who can take care of them instead.

Girls, I must address this next topic. What is this phenomenon that's going around where women are targeting men with good jobs and professions just to have a baby and get paid. I know this has always been done, but today its being taken to a whole new level. I just want to raise one question. Shouldn't the life of a child mean more than a paycheck? Tell me what is the difference between a woman who has a child for the sole purpose of collecting a welfare check vs one who thinks she's better because she collects a check from a man that she has targeted. Please stop using your coochie as supplemental income. Yes, even in the age where women seem to be on top of their game, some women are not being smart. They are always in some sort of financial crisis or predicament where they are not taking care of business.

For the sake of argument, let's say the man is treating you right and his wallet is an open bank vault. Have you thought about the fact that someday he may leave; either through death or for some other reason. Have you saved some of that money that he has given you? Have you invested some of that money that he has given you? Have you prepared adequately for your future? I've seen and read many stories about women who had to move back home with their parents because they spent every dime foolishly. They failed to prepare and plan adequately for their future. Women, let's be smart about our lives, those looks and that body is not going to last forever. God has invested much into making you a strong and intelligent woman, it's too late in the day to be stupid. God bless the child who has her own.

$ CALCULATE THE COST $

What may be the cost of not preparing for your future adequately?:

- Having a man meet all your needs will give you a false sense of security. You think it will always be this way.
- You will eventually be taken off the books; your shelf life is short.
- You will become economically strapped. If you have not taken care of business, you will not be able to get a home loan, nor will you have any retirement, medical, dental, or savings etc.
- Afterthoughts and regrets; wishing you had done things differently. Eventually, you will regret missing all the opportunities that you did not take advantage of when you had the chance.
- As time passes, life will become very hard and stressful if you have not prepared adequately.

A SELAH MOMENT:

Without his income, have you prepared adequately for your future? Are you investing the money that he is giving you wisely?

_____

_____

_____

CHAPTER ELEVEN

The Facts Don't Lie

Do not give a man your heart until he has proven himself.

Take your time and get to know the man that you are with before releasing your emotions. Focus on the **facts** and **not on how you feel**. I do understand that this is a very difficult thing to do especially in the beginning, while in the hot passionate seemingly love struck stage. You will need to pray and ask God for help. When we start focusing on feelings, it is easy to become disillusioned. Feelings will cause you to continue in a bad relationship even in the face of danger. Feelings will make you disregard and overlook issues that may lead to break up and/or divorce down the road. Break up or divorce is never easy, your heart cannot take another hit, so guard it like the precious treasure it is.

Do not give a man your heart until he has proven himself. He has proven that he can be trusted and relied on. He has proven that he has your back. He has proven that he loves you and you know it, not only do you know it, he shows it. **You want qual-**

ity! You want a happy and healthy relationship. Stop falling in love so easily and quickly. Wait! Don't go "all in" if he makes you feel insecure but yet special. You know something is wrong, but you can't put your finger on it. Wait! God is speaking and trying to tell you something that you need to know. Slow down! Stop and listen!

The following scenarios may reveal some FACTS that you may be over looking that will impact your relationship negatively in the future:

The facts show that he has bad spending habits and cannot hold on to his paycheck past a couple of days. He spends his money impulsively and foolishly, especially on big ticket items such as cars and gadgets. Your emotions say this is okay because you are not currently being affected. Know that this type of reckless behavior will put your financial future at risk. Later on, you may think that you have been saving towards your child's education only to discover that Mr. Man has drained the educational fund and bought a new car. This type of behavior, if left unchecked, will cause you to incur a lot of debt, which will eventually result in undue anxiety, stress, and strain on the relationship. Statistics show that financial issues are one of the top three causes of divorce and discord in relationships.

The facts show that he is not going to marry you. After dating for one year, he still doesn't want to talk about where the relationship is going. Your emotions say it's cool because you don't want to put pressure on him. His lack of conversation about this subject is telling you that he is not even thinking about committing to you any time soon, if at all. He says you are the one for him and he wants to marry you. Be careful, he may just be saying that to keep you on the hook as long as he can. A man who is ready for marriage will not be afraid to have conversations about marriage with you especially after dating you for one year.

The facts show that he does not spend time with you the way a man who is really into you should. He calls or comes over whenever he has time which is usually once or maybe twice every other week; however, it is not enough to meet your need. Your emotions say it's okay because he's working long and hard hours. When a man is really into and loves a woman, he will **find** the time to call and come over.

The facts show that he is not attentive to your needs, you have to coerce him to do simple things for you, he doesn't want to touch you the way a man who is really into you should, but you say it's okay because men really don't show their affections anyways. You cannot love without giving. Love and giving go hand in hand. If a man is telling you that he loves you but is not giving to you, pump your brakes, **something vital is missing** in this relationship.

The facts show that he is hot headed and drinks too much. Your emotions say it's okay because he has never been violent toward me, I am careful not to make him angry; besides, he is really good to me and my children. Deep down on the inside, you know he is a ticking time bomb, and you need to get out because your time is coming. If he is hot headed, he will eventually become violent toward you also.

The facts show that he is violent and abusive. He hit you, but he said he would never do it again. Your emotions say, it's okay, he will not do it again, I am partly to blame. A man like this has anger-management issues and has not learned to discipline his temper. He will definitely hit you again. You are not the first woman that he has hit, so why do you believe him when he says he won't do it again? Has he received any type of intervention to help him deal with his problem? Nope, I guess not. Girls, I can't believe that we are still falling for this line. It has been proven time after time, if he hits you once, he will hit you again.

The facts show that you have caught him at least two times with another woman. Your emotions say that you are the main woman and the other woman means nothing to him, it's just sex. He loves me and not her; all the while your stomach is in knots, you can't sleep, your soul is in turmoil, and you have no peace. Deep down on the inside, you know you need to let it go, but you keep holding on, hoping he will love you like he used to. If the man is not sincere and thinks or knows that you are weak for him, he will continue to disrespect you with woman after woman. A woman should never tolerate a man's bad behavior. If you take him back, make sure he has earned the right to be there. A man who is truly ready for commitment, knows there is not anything worthwhile in those streets, the true blessing is what he has at home.

The facts show that he is a show off, trying to be impressive. Whenever he goes out, he is a big spender and dresses very well, even though he doesn't have the money to do either. He is always strapped for cash and expects you to pick up the slack. And, he gets angry and accuses you of not having his back if you refuse. Your emotions say, "It's okay because he is a real, real, great guy and this is the only problem that we have in our relationship." Sweetie Sweets, this is a big problem. Many marriages/relationships end due to financial issues. There is an old adage that says, "When poverty comes in at the door, love flies out the window." If you and your man are talking marriage, you should definitely talk finances.

Please remember: The purpose of the dating process is to get to know him. This is the time to critically evaluate whether this relationship is right for you or not. Take your time and get to know the person that you are with. **Texting and talking on the phone does not qualify as quality time** needed in order to get to know someone. Men have been known to have a wife and kids, while building a virtual relationship with you via phone and web. Spending time will bring clarity, especially if there are some concerns or doubts. Please do not go into denial and ignore the facts and be like that ostrich burying her head in the sand. Marriage is a very important decision not to be taken lightly or handled irresponsibly. It is by far one of the most important decision that you will make in your lifetime, so make it carefully. Getting to know a person **TAKES TIME.**

$ CALCULATE THE COST $

What may be the costs of making decisions about your relationship based solely on your emotions?

- Decisions based solely upon emotions are risky because feelings often change.

- Decisions based solely upon emotions could cloud your judgment because you are so focused on the potential of who he could become, rather than focusing on who he actually is. The more intense your feelings, the more misleading your judgment could become.

- Decisions based solely upon emotions will blind your eyes and cause you not to see all of those blaring red flags.

- Decisions based solely upon emotions will not allow you to see the facts as they really are. If you continue in a relationship laden with an issue or issues, you could develop unhealthy coping skills such as an addiction.

- Decisions based solely upon emotions could place you in victim status because of your inability to face and confront your relationship issues. When you do not confront, you give up your power to create a relationship that you will actually enjoy. You do not confront because you fear that you may actually need to end the relationship, even though that may be the best thing for you to do.

A SELAH MOMENT:

Are you truly calculating the cost of how this relationship will affect you in the future? Are you seeing the facts as they really are, or as you want them to be? Is your judgment clouded because you are so emotionally attached to this individual?

He has an addiction, and gets really aggressive with you after he's been drinking and/or drugging? What price will you have to pay to stay in this relationship?

_____

_____

_____

CHAPTER TWELVE

You Might Not Know Yourself as Well as You Think You Do

Why are we settling for relationships that offer us so little?

When you are with your girls, ya'll talk about it. And you say you see the signs, the red flags, yet you go ahead and get involved with, get engaged to and marry him anyways. What causes us to always overlook the obvious?

He is never there. He is married to his job. You are always lonely. Whenever he comes home from work, he is so tired and wants to be left alone or he will go and do something that he enjoys. It's all about him. You feel really insecure in this relationship. You feel that he is going through a temporary phase and he will eventually want to spend more time with you like he used to. You must realize that your relationship has changed. Somehow you overlook the signs and refuse to see the obvious.

He never takes you out on a date; and if you do go out, it's at your expense and at your suggestion. All he ever wants to do; is come over, eat, and mount up. You are happy with the fact that you have someone in your life that you enjoy being with. You feel that with time; he will make the perfect husband, especially if you can pray for him and get him involved in the church. Somehow you overlook the signs and refuse to see the obvious.

He is a habitual liar. You've already caught him in several lies. You are absolutely embarrassed by his lying and know that one day it will lead to big trouble. However, his personality is so charming and you guys have a lot in common. You think that your relationship will last because you guys are highly compatible and he is the only man who truly understands who you are. Somehow you overlook the signs and refuse to see the obvious.

He told you he would never hit you again, this is the umpteenth time that he's done it, and you knew he beat the other girlfriend before you, yet you overlook the signs and refuse to see the obvious.

He is extremely possessive and jealous. He's constantly questioning and checking your every move. Every moment of your free time is spent with him to the point that family and friends are shut out of your life. His jealousy makes you feel nervous, however you adore all the attention that he gives you. Somehow you overlook the signs and refuse to see the obvious.

Much of what our friends, family, and even this book is telling you, will fall on deaf ears because for whatever reason, our situation is going to be different. The good book says, "we are ever learning and never able to come to the knowledge of the truth." In other words, yes you acknowledge the truth with your words, but you do not act upon that truth. However, your ability to act upon that truth may be blocked by strong needs, strong desires, self-deception, illusions, and delusions etc.

Girlfriends, **denial is self-defeating behavior**. When you live in denial you are working against your own best interest. Denial prevents you from taking the appropriate actions and ultimately creating the situation that is best for you.

> Case and point: Nikki was in a relationship with a man that she absolutely loved and adored. Initially, they spent much quality time together and she left his presence feeling satisfied and complete. Then, they started spending less time together because he went back to school. As a matter of fact, Nikki was paying for part of his education. The time spent together and phone calls became less and less.
>
> Nikki thought that this behavior was okay because it was the natural progression of Mr. Dude taking on more responsibilities. The only time that he called, was when he needed something. He called once per month to discuss all the bills that she had agreed to help him pay. They never saw each other anymore. Nikki knew that Mr. Dude had more time available than what he was letting on because he would talk about activities that he did with family and friends. She was never invited. This type of behavior went on and on for months.
>
> Nikki rationalized that his actions were okay because if she could just hold on a little while longer; his schooling would soon be over, they would be married, and she would reap the rewards of her investment. If she could hang in there a little longer, things were going to turn

around. Nikki thought that if she pulled out now, she was going to miss her blessing.

Mr. Dude began to ask for more and he gave less. And when Nikki confronted him about their issue, it became a big ordeal that led to an argument. He would say, "You know what I'm trying to do, this is for us." Everybody except Nikki, could see that this situation was not working in her favor. Of course, the situation never turned around until she decided to put an end to it. By then, she had wasted much time and squandered hundreds of dollars that she could have saved for herself and her children.

Nikki should have ended that relationship as soon as Mr. Man stopped spending any time with her. Like many women, Nikki was guilty of having too much patience, staying in a bad relationship far too long. She also allowed herself to become a reckless and foolish giver; which means she continued to invest in a relationship that offered her nothing but an empty promise of what life would be like once Mister finished school. Nikki ignored all the facts. Relationship problems usually go from bad to worse until you address the issue.

One of the greatest gifts you can give yourself is to get to know yourself on the deepest level possible. You might ask, what is the benefit of getting to know yourself deeply? Getting to know yourself deeply will help you to discover the core of who you are. It will help you develop an acute awareness of your feelings and needs at all times. It will help you to locate yourself and know the truth about why you are choosing who you are choosing to be in a relationship with.

It is a dangerous thing to not know what is driving you to make the choices that you make. In other words, examine the reasons why you are with him. Are you with him because he has money and status? Are you with him because all of your friends are now married and you want to be married too? Are you with him because you don't want to return back to that dry place of spending all your weekends alone or with the girlfriends that you are sick of?

Are you with him because you think this is the best you can do? Are you with him because you think it ain't no mo' good men left, it took a long time to get this half way decent brother so I better try and make this relationship work? The point I am trying to make is, spend some me time, examining the true reason why you are with a person; especially if the person is treating you poorly. Did you connect with and stay with him because of an unhealthy need?

Getting to know yourself and why you are choosing to stay in an unhealthy relationship will stop you from being tricked by your own needs. It will stop you from going out and grabbing Mr. Right Now and trying to turn him into Mr. Forever. We never want to admit to ourselves the times when we are desperately lonely. Most people are so out of touch with themselves they don't even know they are operating from a place of deprivation and unfulfilled needs.

Case and point: I had a coworker who had not had the company of a man for approximately ten years. She went out on the dating scene and did not have much success so she decided to date online. Great, I thought, at least she is trying and not giving up. After about two weeks, she met someone. She told me he was not what she really wanted. She just needed somebody to go out with and talk to on the phone; you know, something to look forward to when she got home. I said, be careful girl, you know your love tank is pretty empty and when you're hungry, you'll eat from the trash can.

She assured me she just wanted to have a little fun. Well, two weeks later, she was talking about this might be the one. Dude was a musician, with an unstable income. He smoked weed like crazy. He had only taken her out twice, they had done most of their dating on the phone. However, he made her feel really good emotionally. Two years later, she was still talking to dude on the phone telling me that one day they were going to be married. Within that two years, they may have gone out about four times. She was devastated and surprised when she found out he was going to be married to another woman.

What caused her not to see that he was just stringing her along; to all of us looking on, it was obvious. Why did she not examine herself to see why she settled for a relationship that offered her *so* little?

I understand why we stay in relationships with failure and trouble written all over it. We see the good in him. We become addicted to the hope of God changing things. After all, sister so and so's husband was like that, and look at him now, he is really wonderful. If you only knew half the hell that sister went through, you would run as fast as you can and head for the hills. Our problem is that we focus so much on the moment that we forget about the future.

We believe that if we work at it, and pray about it, eventually our change will come. There is only one problem in this equation. He ain't workin' at it, he ain't pray'n' about it, he doesn't want to change. You are the only one doing all the work. Remember, it takes two to successfully make a relationship work. If you marry him, you will get more of the same and even worse. When are you going to start loving yourself enough to believe God for the man who will love you truly?

Who convinced you that you cannot get or have better? You got the man who you are with didn't you? Believe me, if he wanted you, someone else will too. You are a good woman and you deserve the best. If you are not where you should be, then become the best you can possibly be. Go back to school and get that career. Take the time to dress and groom yourself with style. Please don't tell me money is an issue. If it is, get your hair and nails done at a beauty college. Go to a second hand store or discount store to buy clothes. You will find unbelievable deals there. You invest in everybody else, why not invest in yourself? You are worth it. If your attitude is bad, then ask the good Lord to help you get it right.

Denial also keeps us from recognizing internal issues that we need to deal with. You need to admit to yourself, that part of you may be broken, and needs to be rebuilt. It's okay if you are broken! It is NOT okay to stay broken. Do you suffer from abandonment issues that cause you to be clingy and stay in a bad relationship too long because you don't want to be left alone? Do you attach yourself to men who are abrasive, rude, and outspoken because you can not speak up for yourself? Do you connect with men who you know will never be enough, because it will take too much work to connect with the one you really want?

Many of us do not even know that we are broken because we do not practice the art of self-evaluation. I refer to self-evaluation as getting to know yourself on the deepest level.

You might ask, how do I even start to get to know myself deeply? You start by facing those places in your life where you are weak; those places in your life that you want to avoid and not look at. You admit to yourself when you are lonely, needy, desperate etc. You spend some much needed time alone and with God, getting to know yourself. The more you get to know God, the more you will get to know yourself.

During this time you are asking yourself pertinent questions such as why do I really want to be with dude? Is he good for me and my children?

Pray and ask God to help you see the truth, know the truth, believe the truth, and accept the truth. Ask the Lord to give you the strength to do what is right for you. Try really hard to not allow self-denial to keep you from the beautiful life and love that you so awesomely deserve.

A word of caution: If you have not been in a relationship for two to fifteen plus years, your love tank is empty and you may be vulnerable and a prime candidate for self-deception and denial. I am pretty sure that you will disagree with and deny this statement ☺.

$ CALCULATE THE COST $

What may be the cost of not knowing yourself deeply?

- You could become more vulnerable to deception.
- Not knowing yourself deeply could cause you not to deal in reality about your relationship. You continuously lie to yourself and go into denial about how bad your relationship really is.
- Living in denial may cause you to be isolated from your support group. You will not listen to your friends and family when they try to help you, especially when dealing with an abusive and controlling man.
- Your self-esteem could suffer long term damages which would eventually affect your confidence and undermine your everyday performance and success in life. For example, you were once an A or B student, now you are flunking out of school.
- Not knowing yourself deeply could cause you to have repetitive patterns of choosing people that will not benefit you.

A SELAH MOMENT:

Have you developed an acute awareness of your feelings and needs at all times? Do you know what is driving you to be in this relationship with your man? What are the reasons why you are really with him?

_____

_____

_____

CHAPTER THIRTEEN

Stay in Your Own House

A woman's place is never inside another woman's home.

An older woman once told me, "A woman's place is never inside another woman's home." If a man has a wife or is in a committed relationship **LEAVE HIM ALONE! YES, I AM SCREAMING AT YOU!**

Think about the pain that you felt when your man left you for another. You know the struggle, you know the pain. Stop the cycle. Kids need their dads! Wives need their husbands! You need your husband! Your children need their daddy!

I am always amazed at the women who break up other folks' relationships, then when it happens to them, they are surprised. And, not only surprised, they are devastated.

REALLY? Be careful, be very, very, careful about what you do to other people. When karma comes, it is nothing nice. The Word of God puts it like this, "Be not deceived; God is not mocked:

For whatsoever a man soweth, that shall he also reap." In other words, if you did it to her, it **WILL** be done to you.

What has happened to us as women, as sisters? There was a time when we had respect for another woman's home, at minimum we felt real bad about breaking it up. Now, home wreck'n' is what's trend'n'. It's beginning to be the cool and acceptable thing to do, to take another woman's man. Sisters are even taking pride in taking another woman's man. We've developed the attitude, well someone took mine, so I'm gonna take hers. We have developed the attitude that all men cheat, so if you can't beat 'em then join 'em. When are we going to stop hurting each other and start caring about each other?

If we are going to make it as a nation, this country needs strong families. Please remember that it's the hand that rocks the cradle that rules the world. One of the greatest assignments that a woman has in the earth is to bring forth a man or woman of God. Are you raising your children to have a standard? What kind of example are you setting before your children? Do your sons and your daughters see you with this man and with that one? Do your children see you with your best friend's man or cheating with other women's husbands or boyfriends? Are you raising your children to be reckless, careless, and irresponsible about their lives and the lives of others? Selah-which means to calmly sit and think about this.

Another thing that I must address is you being friends with a married man. There is nothing wrong with being friends with a married man **AND his wife;** however, there must be boundaries there. For argument's sake, let's say that you and Mr. Man were really good friends before he got married. If you and your buddy used to talk everyday two to three times a day, you have to severely cut back.

Yes, your relationship **MUST** change because your presence may be preventing him from developing intimacy with his wife. Marriage is between two people not three. Think about it, if it was you, and your husband was spending more time with his "friend" than with you. You would feel slighted and have a problem with it. He calls and checks on his friend more than he checks on you. This is selfish and disrespectful on part of the man and the friend.

If you really care about your friend, you would also care that he develops a happy and healthy marriage with his wife by not allowing him to continue leaning on you for the emotional support that he should be getting from his wife. This type of relationship will make any wife jealous or feel insecure because the friend is holding the place that she should have.

$ CALCULATE THE COST $

What may be the cost of infidelity?

- Take a good look at how he is treating his wife, because if you marry him, her life will become your life. You will not escape Karma.

- Realize that if you make that step outside of your marriage, home will never be the same.

- This type of relationship is very risky and can be a life altering event. Matters of the heart are tricky and can turn a sane person crazy. I personally know of a man who found out that his wife was cheating and came home and killed himself and the kids. My God, what a price to pay! You don't want to end up on the television show Snapped.

- Please realize that you are only a part-time lover. Yes, it is safe to assume that he is still having sex with his wife.
- Realize that as the other woman, you are experiencing the best of times with him, but once you marry him, the reality of relationship troubles will kick in, just like it did with his current marriage. Paradise will end and reality will begin.
- As the other woman, if he dies or leaves, his material wealth will go to his wife and children. You will be left with nothing in the end; especially if you have invested many years of your life into this man.

A SELAH MOMENT:

If you have a husband and you are happy, would you want another woman to come in and break up your home? Why do you feel it's alright to break up hers?

_____

_____

_____

CHAPTER FOURTEEN

Beware of the Bad Boy

According to many women that I have talked to, dating bad boys can be exciting, challenging, and just down right fun. They are often handsome and fine as heck. They are erotic and can make love like nobody's business. They are the ultimate protector and exudes power, confidence, and control. However, the truth of the matter is, you cannot build a lasting relationship based on eroticism, lust, and a good time.

Bad boys are known to be womanizers. Bad boys are known to be abusive. Yet, they are a highly sought after commodity amongst many women. Women dreamy-eyedly have told me that they want a man who is rebellious, one who goes against the grain and have a bit of a criminal element to them. They've told me how bored they are with a man who is considered a good boy, and at the same time, telling me how miserable they are because they are being mistreated by their bad boy. Girls, Girls, Girls, we need to get our heads on straight. Make choices that align with who you really are and what you really want out of life and out of your relationship.

To my sisters who have made up in their minds that they love being with the bad boy type of man no matter what, and still want to proceed with the relationship: if you can, I need you to hear me. Please be sure to calculate the cost before moving forward because dating this type of man could change the course of your life forever. I am asking you to really, really, THINK your decision over carefully before you continue on, and be ready for whatever consequences that may come as a result of your decision. Please remember that you are not an island, and that your child/children, your family, your friends, and all the people that you love will be affected by the decisions that you make.

$ CALCULATE THE COST $

What may be the cost of dating a bad boy?

- You will begin to become like him; rather than you changing him, he will change you. If you find yourself becoming a bad girl for your bad boy, get out of that relationship and get out NOW! Bad behavior always corrupts good behavior.

- Endanger your life by putting you in high risk situations. He may want you to take part in a crime, and make you feel guilty if you say no. If you take part, you are putting yourself and everyone that you love in real danger. Please don't end up on one of the TV shows Investigation ID, Snapped, or For My Man.

- You are a means to an end. Each of his women serve a purpose. Perhaps you are the one who gives him money or maybe you are the one to provide a place for him to crash whenever he is in your part of the town.

You only have him the moment that he is with you. You can be replaced at any given moment; especially if you are good to him and fall in love with him.

- He plays games. He knows how to manipulate your emotions. If he screws up for any reason and you confront him, he will always twist things around to make you feel like it was all your fault. He hardly takes responsibility for anything he does, no matter how bad he hurts you. He always expects you to put up with his crap and not complain.

- If you hook up with him, you can look forward to poverty. This type of man, normally ain't goin' nowhere with his life. He has no goals and no direction. He is highly unproductive; he parties all night and sleeps all day.

- He certainly is not a good role model for your children to be around. Please tell me that you did not move him in with your children. This type of person is too risky of a person for your child/children to be around.

- Being with him could be emotionally damaging for you and your children that may take years to recover from, if ever; especially if you are going in and out of relationships and exposing your child/children to every man that you emotionally attach yourself to.

- He is usually a rebel and involved in illegal activity.

- You and your children do not matter. He is utterly selfish and it's all about him. You and your kids will be 2nd or 3rd or whatever place he has for you in his life.

Be ready to fight and have a life filled with drama. Bad boys usually have a temper, and have little to no control over their emotions. You will more than likely become his punching bag whenever things are messed up in his world.

If your goal is to have a meaningful relationship that will ultimately lead to a good marriage, this is NOT your guy.

CHAPTER FIFTEEN

Pay Attention: Turn Down the Sound and Look at the Picture

You must learn to read a man's actions.

His words say, "I am a man," but his actions show he is still a boy.

His words say, "I love you and you mean the world to me," but his actions show you are not a priority in his life.

His words say, "Girl, I got you," but his actions show he is never there when you need him.

His words say, "You are number one," however, he does not respond to your text or phone calls until way late in the day, if at all.

His words say, "I really want to spend more time with you," but his actions show he'd rather spend more time with his friends.

The true identity of a person is revealed by what he does and not by what he says. Words mean nothing if they are not backed by actions. There must be consistency which means words and actions must line up. There must be reciprocity if a relationship is going to be healthy, lasting, and strong. When love is present, it is expressed both in word and deed. Well, you might say that he loves me. He just doesn't know how to show it. Wrong! Love knows how to behave. Love is an action word and will compel him to show it.

A man must be able to meet your genuine needs. What do I mean by genuine needs? Genuine needs are things or actions that you need your partner to do more than anything else. These actions cause you to feel secure and sure about the relationship. For example, maybe he hardly calls; once every three days is good enough for him, but not for you. You genuinely **need** to hear your honey's voice every day even if just for five minutes. You enjoy connecting with him, this makes you feel secure and sure of the relationship. When a man is interested and into you, he will do those things that will cause you to feel secure. If a man is not calling and coming to see you in the way that you need him to, he is **not available** to meet your genuine needs. And at the end of the day, you still DO NOT have a boyfriend, you are still very much alone even though you are in a "relationship."

One of the main reasons you got a boyfriend is for companionship, so that you would not have to spend your weekends alone. And, to have someone to look forward to talking to. If you are still spending the majority of your weekends alone, then this guy is not meeting your genuine needs. Oh yeah, "but babe I am working real hard, you know my hours." If his work is interfering with his availability, then he is not ready to be in a relationship because relationships require time. A man who is really into you will **make time** to see you. I don't care how busy he is. At the end of the day, you still DO NOT have a boyfriend, you are still very much alone even though you are in a "relationship."

Turn down the sound and look at the picture, stop justifying his bad behavior. Yes, you see what you think you see. We must wake up and look at his actions, and at what's really going on rather than listening to our daydreams, our fantasies, our emotions or "stepping out on faith." You must learn how to read a man's actions.

A lot of times a man will put you on rations. What are rations? He is giving you just enough to keep you holding on. If he has you on rations, then one of two things is happening. You are either his transitional girl until he finds the one he really wants or he is juggling; trying to spend time with you and someone else.

You think that if you love him better, if you love him harder, he will eventually return that same love to you. No! What normally happens is, if he stays, he will give you less and less. He will become even more selfish because he knows you will be there no matter what. Baby girl, move on and stop accepting less than what you deserve.

Also, pay close attention to what a man is "supposed to say," but doesn't. What a man doesn't say is just as important as what he says.

Case and Point: I was with this guy and we were to be married. I went to his family reunion and he introduced me as his brother's sister-in-law. That spoke volumes to me, and I started backing my emotions up immediately. When I called him on the carpet, he said, "Oh, they all know, look at what I did after that, I grabbed you and pulled you under my arm." Really? About a month after that, I discovered that he was cheating and ended the relationship.

Some signs to look for that may indicate that you may need to take a closer look at the picture:

- You just got out of the hospital and he never came to see you.
- You've been in a relationship for some time, he's still spending time with you, but there is a disconnect. Things are sort of the same, but his pattern and his behavior has changed. He has always made you feel like number one, now you no longer do. Look out! There may be a third player on board.
- He lives out of state and the two of you have been talking on the phone for a while now. He is telling you how he wants to be with you and is making plans to move where you are. You have a business trip to his city and would like to see him. You inform him of this and he agrees to pick you up. On the day of your arrival, he is ghost. He is not answering your calls and Lawd knows he never showed to pick you up. And, he had the nerve to call you when you got back home.
- He is ghost on all special holidays and weekends. You don't see him for Christmas, Thanksgiving, or Valentine's Day; until a day or two afterward. He sent a text though, to let you know he was thinking about you.

> Things have been going really good between the two of you and all of a sudden he is ghost. No phone calls and no return calls. He just shows back up on the scene expecting to pick up where ya'll left off.

It is too late in the day for you to continue trying to figure out where you stand in a relationship. If you are patient and observant, you will find out everything you need to know without asking him a thing. Put more value on what he does than what he says. Be very clear, upfront, and honest TO YOURSELF (most importantly) and to Mister about your needs. If he steps up to the plate then great! If he does not, be true to you, maintain your boundaries and keep it moving. If he is a worthy man, he may leave but will come back later and treat you with the honor and respect you so deserve.

$ CALCULATE THE COST $

What may be the cost of not paying attention?

- Not paying attention will cause you to make poor decisions. Use your attention as a valuable resource to help you make better dating and marriage choices.

- Not paying attention will cause you to waste your time. If you are forty plus years old, time becomes a precious commodity. Some men only come into your life to waste your time. We always want to believe that we should give a person the benefit of the doubt. Sometimes the benefit of the doubt may be deserved, but most of the time it is not.

- Not paying attention will cause you to ignore important details about the relationship that may indicate there's a third player on board; in other words, he's in another relationship.

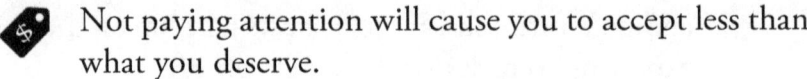 Not paying attention will cause you to accept less than what you deserve.

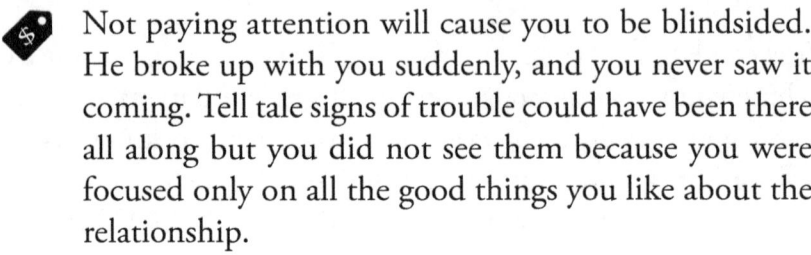 Not paying attention will cause you to be blindsided. He broke up with you suddenly, and you never saw it coming. Tell tale signs of trouble could have been there all along but you did not see them because you were focused only on all the good things you like about the relationship.

A SELAH MOMENT:

Are his actions consistent with his words?

Are there any behaviors and beliefs that you may be ignoring, signaling that you are wasting your time or that will possibly cause the relationship to fail in the future?

Are you still trying to figure out where you stand in this relationship? If so, are you waiting for him to define the relationship rather than you taking charge to figure out whether or not you are investing your time and emotions with the right guy?

_____

_____

_____

CHAPTER SIXTEEN

Mind Time

If you are on a man's mind, he will be compelled to call and spend time with you, he will not be able to help himself.

What is mind time you might ask? Mind time is when a person becomes the center of your world. Your every waking thoughts revolve around that person. Your day is filled with thoughts of their smile. You aim to please and you are fulfilled and satisfied by all that you do to make them happy. In other words, he's in your head and you can't get him out. It's almost like you are obsessing over him.

A girlfriend of mine met a guy and after two months of dating, he told her how he had her back. "Girl, I got you," those words resonated with her spirit. He told her all the wonderful things a girl wanted to hear. He went away to see his kids and was gone for about two weeks. He did not call or text her. I said to her, "Girl, dude is not really that into you if you have not heard from him at all. Not even a text?" I told her, "He aint giving you no mind time." Of course she disagreed and gave me some weird ole excuse as to why she had not heard from him.

If a man that you are with, goes away and does not call, something is vitally wrong. He is for sure not giving you any mind time. If you are in a man's head, he will be COMPELLED to call, he can't help himself.

As women, we are constantly asking the question, I wonder how he feels about me. Does he really like me? If he's not calling, more than likely his interest is not that strong. If he doesn't want to spend time with you, more than likely his interest is definitely not that strong.

Do yourself a favor and force yourself to stop thinking about him. Remove his phone number so that you will not continue to call him. DO NOT call him again until he calls you. Continue busying yourself dating other prospects. A man who is into you will stay in touch. If he texts or calls you just to say hello, to see how your day is going, or to say good morning and goodnight; it is a clear sign that he thinks about you often and wants you to know it. However, we are still going to proceed with caution and take things slowly just in case there is an ulterior motive.

$ CALCULATE THE COST $

What may be the cost of you giving a man too much mind time?

 Your attraction will increase for a man who is not into you. If you continue to think about him, you will stay attached to him and unable to move on quickly.

- If he is not showing much interest, and you do not move on quickly, you will begin to think that something is wrong with you as to why he is not responding to you. After all, you felt the power of the connection. If there is a real connection, he will put in the effort and the time.

- If you give him too much mind time, you will over think every moment that you guys connected and drive yourself crazy, wondering if he likes you or not. Know that he doesn't like you enough to create time and space for you in his world.

- If you give him too much mind time, you will fall for the fantasy guy: the guy that you created in your head, and not the man he actually is. You will create a relationship that does not exist.

- You are wasting valuable time by continuing to think about him; waiting and hoping that he calls. Next! Move on!

A SELAH MOMENT:

Are you giving too much mind time to a man who is not that in to you? Is he calling and spending time with you the way he should be?

___

___

___

CHAPTER SEVENTEEN

Investing Your Goodness and Getting Nothing in Return

There must be reciprocity if a relationship is going to last.

In a relationship it is important to gauge what you are giving in relation to what you are receiving. If you are the one doing all the giving, the sacrificing, and the loving, you don't have a true relationship; you don't even have a good friendship. If you are the one doing the majority of the calling, the one suggesting that we need to spend more time together, the one waiting for him to show up. If you are the one making sure he has a nice gift on all special occasions, while he either forgets yours or buys you nothing at all, not even a card. Eventually you will become frustrated, drained, and feel used. You cannot continue to sacrifice your needs and put them on hold and get little to nothing in return.

A major mistake that most of us girls make when it comes to love, is not receiving love in proportion to what we are giving. If you are going to have a healthy and satisfying relationship, both people will need to make an investment of their time, emotions, and finances etc. It takes TWO, THE BOTH OF YOU, in order to create a satisfying and strong relationship, both people have to take full responsibility for the relationship.

It is easy to deceive ourselves into thinking that if we love harder, sacrifice more, keep ourselves looking good, and have their backs etc., that somehow our partner will see that we are that good woman that we've heard him and other men say they want. We as women, give and give and give; and, there is nothing wrong with that, IF there is reciprocity. There must be reciprocity, if the relationship is going to last, be strong and satisfying.

If you are an over-giver, pull back and put some boundaries in place. Stop investing all your goodness and getting little to nothing in return. You don't have to sit down and talk to him about repetitive issues that plague the relationship again, because you have already done that a thousand times already. Sometimes it's better to show him than tell him. It is not too late to show that you have standards.

If he becomes intrigued and wants to talk about moving forward and makes the adjustments then great! You can start all over again and create the loving connection that you want and desire. If he bounce, let him go and remove his number from your phone so that you will not call him again. DO NOT call him or accept him back without boundaries or his willingness to work at the relationship and make the needed changes. The fact that he left, leaves no doubt, that he is not ready for or mature enough to establish a healthy and satisfying relationship. Many times a man returns back because he ran out of options, or things just did not work out with the other woman. Maintaining your boundaries will ensure that he is back for the right reasons. Keeping him accountable will either drive him or draw him, meaning accountability will either drive him away from you or drive him to be closer to you.

Believe me, if you accept him back without boundaries, he will suck the life out of you. Your relationship will become toxic, like poison to your soul which will eventually effect your future relationships. In other words, because of his rejection, you will begin to doubt yourself. Your self-esteem will be lowered, placing you in a position to settle for men who are not worthy of you. Stop investing your love into a man who does not love, respect, and give to you in the same way you give to him.

Love will not flourish and grow where there is a lack of reciprocity. The chances of you developing a healthy, wholesome, and wonderful relationship where there is no reciprocity will be next to impossible. Let him go! Leave him alone, and wait for the one who will love you like you deserve to be loved. The one who will love you truly is out there and will come. Believe it!

$ CALCULATE THE COST $

What may be the cost of you investing your goodness and getting nothing in return?

- You are cheating yourself. You will be the one coming up short because he invests little or nothing into the relationship.
- You are setting yourself up to collect more baggage. You will eventually become emotionally abused and neglected if things do not quickly change.
- You put yourself at risk to be used.

- When loving and giving is out of balance, you will eventually build up resentment and frustration towards that person.
- The relationship will be working for only him, and not the both of you.

A SELAH MOMENT:

Are you an over-giver? Who is taking care of you? Is it time to put some boundaries in place, or is it time to cut your losses and leave?

___

___

___

CHAPTER EIGHTEEN

I Will Take a Chance

Marriage is not a decision that we should gamble with.

God says yes to His will, not yours. Many times women hook up with men they should not be with because they believe they can pray him through. After all, prayer changes thangs. Still other women may feel that they have a special kind of love for a man, that with their help and support, he will change for the better. You **KNOW** he has major issues and is not ready for a relationship.

If God impressed in your spirit that this is not the right guy for you, but you persist and go on with the relationship anyways, God is not obligated to bless it. The Lord said, "Whom **I** put together let no man put asunder." Yes, God is rich in mercy and may turn some situations around; however, God is not blessing every situation. Some situations you will have to endure because you did not listen to God's voice in the first place.

Could it be that many of our marriages and relationships are not lasting because we are ignoring God's voice?

Why do we pray and ask God, He tells us and we do what we want to do anyways. And, we have the nerve to turn around and throw a fit if God does not bless our union.

I know you love him and want to get married, however, our Heavenly Father knows what and who is best for us. Marriage is not a decision that we should gamble with. We should not have the attitude that I will take my chances, hope, and pray that everything turns out all right.

There was a time when I was immature and wanted Mr. Wonderful more than anything. My eyes were open wide shut. I saw all the red flags, but ignored them. I am a prayer warrior and know that if I can pray effectually and fervently, that my prayers will avail much. However, deep in my heart, I knew that God was saying no, but somehow I convinced myself that he would bless the relationship anyways. I prayed and I prayed and I prayed. But, my marriage did not succeed. Mr. Wonderful turned into Mr. Terrible. My heart was so sad and I remember my Heavenly Father so sweetly saying to me, "This is the moment I was trying to save you from." God's noes are just as important as his yeses. Now, when God says no, I listen and do what He says.

I learned to pray this prayer over myself when I want something really badly, and maybe you can too: Lord speak past my emotions, speak past my desires, and let me truly see, hear, and do what is best in this situation for my life, in Jesus name Amen.

$ CALCULATE THE COST $

What may be the costs of taking a chance when you KNOW better?

 The relationship may not be blessed.

- The odds for divorce becomes higher when you gamble the decision of who you will marry.
- If you move forward, you will do so at your own risk. You may be without Divine protection.
- You may be holding on to something that will distract you from fulfilling your true purpose.
- You will be putting yourself through unnecessary pain, blaming everybody else but yourself.

A SELAH MOMENT:

Are you trying to negotiate with God to get Him to change His mind, so that you can get who you want, however, it is not who He wants for you?

_____

_____

_____

CHAPTER NINETEEN

Doing What Seems Crazy

Dare to trust God even when it seems to be to your disadvantage.

I was engaged to a man who was engaged to another woman while being engaged to me. I was devastated when I found out. It was a pain like I've never felt before. With mass anger and scorn, I poured out my heart before God in prayer. One night, I was sitting in my chair replaying all the scenes in my head of the signs that I should have seen but missed. The Holy Spirit spoke and said, "The goals and dreams that you had for your relationship with him, I want you to pray that she (the other woman) will have them."

I BURST INTO A WAIL! ARE YOU KIDDING ME? Big crocodile tears began to flow. I felt not only betrayed by the ex-fiancé, but now by God. And before I could reason myself out of doing what was asked, I began to pray for their relationship and that God would bless and prosper it. I asked God to bless them to have a happy marriage. Every dream I had dreamed and hoped for with my ex, I asked God to make it happen for her. When I got up off my knees, all the deep intense hurt and pain I felt broke. Something lifted in my spirit. I felt free. God began to heal my heart. What happened within my soul was absolutely miraculous. I was able to move on and let go without bitterness and resentment, or the constant tormenting visuals of them living a happy life together.

There was also another time in my life that God asked me to do something that in my mind was absolutely crazy. I was married and my ex-husband was acting a straight up fool. One morning while in intense prayer, laying my case out before God, the ex came in and was getting ready to iron his shirt. The Holy Spirit said "get up and iron his shirt." Again, I broke into tears and said, "Father, excuse me, I am the one being wronged here, I can't believe you just told me to do something nice for this crazy man. Have you seen how he's been treating me lately? He should be the one ironing my shirt." I was angry and thought that God was letting the ex off the hook. I did not obey God's instructions. I often wonder, what would have happened if I did? Would that had been a turning point in our marriage? Who knows? Therefore, it makes no sense to ask God for His help and then ignore what He tells you to do.

God's faithfulness is amazing when we follow his instructions, especially if what He's asking us to do, seems to be to our disadvantage or detriment. All I know is "our ways are not His ways and our thoughts are not His thoughts." And, that God is always at work on our behalf. Dare to obey that hard and seemingly crazy word that your Heavenly Father may ask you to do. Dare to trust that He will pull you through the roughest of all relationship storms. Trust and obey! You will be okay.

$ CALCULATE THE COST $

What may be the cost of not obeying God's voice?

- You could miss out on something important that could be the turning point in your relationship.
- Confusion. It is easy to become confused, when what you desire is greater than God's will. You will actually convince yourself that what you are doing IS God's will.
- You could miss out on Divine timing. The timing of God is just as important as the word received from God, meaning you can do the right thing at the wrong time and still end up with a negative outcome.
- The right decision will not be made when you do not follow Divine guidance.
- Consequences will come as a result of ignoring Divine instruction.

A SELAH MOMENT:

Is the Lord asking you to do a hard thing concerning the relationship that you are in? Is He prompting you to be nice to a person who does not deserve it?

_____

_____

_____

CHAPTER TWENTY

Good Girls, Beware

The attack is designed to take you out emotionally and render you ineffective for Kingdom work.

Good woman BEWARE! The dating scene has changed from that which you once knew. I grew up in a time when it was popular for a man to want a wife and a family. I could go anywhere; a fish fry, gas station, house party, laundry mat, church, and meet a man that was husband material. It was expected that no later than thirty-five, your typical man would be settled, ready to be faithful and commit to a good woman.

Nowadays, I'm talking about older men age 50 and above who are chasing women faster and more furious than a twenty-year-old. Thanks a lot, Viagra. I had no idea about the ruthless games being played. Some of these scoun-bugars will **say** and **do** anything to deceive you. And, if you're not careful, it will look like and feel like the real thing. But thank God for the Holy Spirit and patience. For patience, is the weapon that forces deceit to reveal itself says author Mike Murdock.

The warfare against the women of faith who are dating is ruthless. The devil knows that he cannot get you to stop loving and worshipping Jesus. The enemy knows he cannot steal your salvation, but if he can hit your heart hard enough with disappointment after disappointment, your heart will become cold and lifeless. Some men will stop at nothing to deceive you. The attack is designed to take you out emotionally and render you ineffective for kingdom work. The devil is after that valuable part of you called the soul which is made up of your mind/intellect, your emotions, and your will. For it is the soul that worships God in spirit and in truth.

Good woman BEWARE! Hell has a strategy. The enemy is launching his number one weapon which is deceit against the good woman. Who do you see mostly in the churches holding on to God? Who do you see doing all of the praying? Who do you see fighting relentlessly for the family? If the enemy can take the woman down, then he's got the world. The enemy's attack on the good girl is like I have never seen before. Many men are choosing to marry the whore rather than the good girl. What in the world is going on? Girlfriend, wake up and follow the signs of the time.

I talk to women all the time. I hear their stories, I read their stories. I sit back in the cut and watch their stories. I have lived their stories. I will tell you three true stories about women (the names have been changed to protect the innocent) who were excitedly dating men of faith, who turned out to be anything but that. It changed their lives forever. It was as though they stopped living and died on the spot. Are they still serving God and living life? Yes, but not like before. It's like a light has been taken out. It's like all their hope is gone and they are just going through the motions of life.

Story no. 1

Cindy had met the perfect man, the one she had believed God for all her life. He was a deacon in the church, he seemed to be very devoted to God. What she liked most about him is they would pray together three or four times a week. They spent much quality time together getting to know one another. All her children liked him but one. The child said it's something about him that I just don't like. Everybody ignored the child because there was no evidence to substantiate the dislike. After some time had passed, Mr. Fella had a wonderful business idea that he told Cindy about. Cindy thought it was an awesome idea and she invested most of her savings to help get his business started. There was no hesitation in her mind because this was a man that she trusted with all her heart: and besides that, they were going to be married within the next six months. He had shown himself to be a true man of God that she trusted completely.

Mr. Fella began to spend much time working on the business and less time with her. Cindy thought nothing of it because she understood that starting a business would require much time. One night while Mr. Fella was asleep, Cindy decided to go through his phone. She saw this number that he called every day, so the next day she called the number. A woman answered the phone. Cindy introduced herself and asked the lady who she was and how did she know Mr. Fella. The lady told her that she was engaged to Mr. Fella and that they had been seeing each other for a few years. Cindy informed the lady that she was also Mr. Fella's fiancée.

Cindy confronted Mr. Fella and he said, "That's what you get for being nosy, you had no business going through my phone."

Cindy was absolutely devastated. The pain was far greater than anything you or I could imagine. Cindy literally lost her mind and had to be institutionalized.

Cindy had only known Mr. Fella for ten months. Within ten months, she had invested most of her money, her time, her trust, and above all her heart. She thought it was safe to give her all based on who he presented himself to be. I cannot stress this point enough, pray for discernment and take your time to get to know who a man truly is. To this day, Cindy has not recovered and it has been at least twelve years now. The fervency in which she used to serve God is gone. Her vivacious and spirited personality that friends and family alike were drawn to is gone. The woman that we once knew as Cindy is gone.

Story no. 2

Tomeka (a.k.a. Meek) met a guy that we were all excited about. He was the vice president of a major company. Mr. Man had a great sense of humor, dressed nice, was articulate, and loved to go to church, as a matter of fact he never missed. My girlfriend went out with him and did everything that couples meeting for the first time do. Meek was *so* excited about this guy that she could not contain her happiness and told everybody she met about him. Because Mr. Man was the Vice-President, he worked long hours, but spent every extra moment that he had with Meek. He begged Tomeka to be patient and told her as soon as this major project ended, they would be able to spend more time together. There was absolutely nothing dude would not do for or give Meek. There was absolutely nothing suspicious about dude except he worked a lot. However, they saw each other faithfully on the weekends. He came to her house and she went to his. We just knew that he was the one.

One day Meek was telling a friend of hers about this wonderful man that she had fallen in love with. The friend said, he sounds like someone I know, let me investigate. The friend came back and said, I do know him, and not only that, he is married with children. Because he works a long ways from home, he has an apartment in the city. Tomeka, did her own investigation and found out it was all true, Mr. Man was living a double life. That day, the joyous, funny, spirited woman that I once knew died. She totally disconnected from life. Meek went to work, came home, and went to church. She did not even praise and serve God as exuberantly as she once did. She had stopped living and was now just existing. It has been more than ten years now, and she has never gone out with or mentioned another man's name since.

Story no. 3

This is one of my stories, something that actually happened to me. I met this guy who swept me off my feet. We met at a conference and talked extensively over the phone. By the time, I agreed to go out with him, it felt like I had known him all my life. Our first date was magical. He took me to a gorgeous restaurant in the hills overlooking Los Angeles. He had a beautifully wrapped red satin gift waiting for me. Inside the box, was a carousal that played the song "Somewhere in Time." He said this was one of his favorite movies. He quoted a line from the movie that said "I've waited for you all my life." He said this was a God thing. I felt the same way. He said, "When I was sixteen years old, God showed me my wife in a vision. And when I saw you, I could not believe it, you had the same face as the woman in my vision." As we continued to see each other, Mister said he didn't believe in premarital sex, he wanted to do things God's way. Wow! This was unreal! A true man of God.

Every time I saw Mister, he had a gift for me. He bought me a journal and said, "In this book, I want you to record the history of our relationship so that when we are old, we will pass it down to our favorite grandchild so that he/she will know the history of how this generation began." Girls, I melted like butter. The relationship was off to a fast and wonderful start. I thought nothing of it because a visiting pastor at our church was doing a series titled the "Suddenlies of God." Honey I thought I was in the Suddenlies of God. I thought what was happening was lining up with the Word of God that I was hearing. Then, Mister bought Laker tickets for me and my girlfriends, we sat on the row with the media, we had excellent seats. He also paid for their parking. OMG, my girlfriends were so happy for me and I believe a tad bit jealous too. Mister also had purchased box seat hockey tickets for himself and me.

It was October and New Year's eve was soon approaching, he told me to choose anywhere in the United States that I wanted to go and bring in the New Year. I chose Time Square. He purchased first class airline tickets and made all the reservations. To top it all off, later that month, he handed me some brochures so that we could start shopping for our brand new home. We talked finances, we talked about having children and how we would raise them, we talked about God and how we wanted to serve him. We talked about how he believed in the longevity of marriage because his parents had been married for more than forty years. He asked me to promise him that we would never talk divorce, we would always work things out. We talked about getting married the coming summer. He was a dream come true.

Then it happened, Mister and I had our first argument. The next day, I received the most beautiful breath taking arrangement of roses that I had ever seen. The flowers were so gorgeous that all the girls in the office wanted to know all about him. Where we met, where he worked etc. I told them where he worked and one of the girls had a friend who worked in the same place. She said, I am going to inquire about him. Fine with me. I said.

Baby, the next day, she said, "Guess what, Dude is married." I thought no way, I call him whenever, we see each other whenever. There is no evidence of any other woman being around. She said his wife is visiting her relatives in Europe. She told me things about him that only a person who knows him would know. I still did not believe it. So that night, I called Mister and told him what I had heard. He said, "Absolutely no way." It occurred to me that I had never been to his house. He told me that he had two guy roommates and felt more comfortable at my house: his reason made sense to me. I told him, "Tomorrow we are going to your house."

He said, "No problem. What time do you want me to pick you up?" I said, "Ten thirty a.m." He said, "Okay."

The next day came and no Mister. From that day until now, I have not seen or heard from him.

Oh my God. I could not breathe. It felt like someone had knocked the wind out of me. I took to my bed and could not get up. Then I got mad. I told my girlfriend that I was going to go to his job, break all windows out of his car and put sugar in his gas tank. Then I was going to follow him home and confront him in front of his wife. She began to pray and convinced me to let God deal with him.

I was absolutely nuts. Thank God for praying friends. Why in the world would anyone go through so much trouble to deceive you? To play with your mind and heart like that? Perhaps the enemy thought that I would be so emotionally wrapped up in this guy that he would take my mind captive to the point that I would never recover from the devastating blow. I too would forfeit my call in Christ by being so emotionally damaged that I would be ineffective for kingdom work. Thank God for praying friends, the enemy's plan to take me out failed. I am still moving forward and serving God in a much greater way than before.

There is a major spiritual battle over who will control your soul. The enemy knows that God has your spirit, but he wants to take your soul; for it is your soul that worships God in spirit and in truth. That's why our Father tells us to guard/keep your heart with all diligence for out of it proceeds the issues of life.

He who controls your mind controls your heart. Your heart is very, very valuable; it is the core of where you live. If your heart is damaged and is unhealthy, it effects everything else that you do. It is time to watch and pray like we never have before.

$ CALCULATE THE COST $

What may be the costs of you not guarding your heart and being on the lookout?

- If you do not look out, you will not see the wolf under the sheep's clothing.
- If you do not look out, you may ignore subtle signs or comments that may seem harmless. This oblivion could prevent you from seeing patterns that may lead to danger.
- If you do not look out, you will not be able to see the forest for the trees; meaning that you have allowed yourself to become too close to this man, no matter what he does, you will not allow yourself to see the truth.
- If you do not guard your heart, you could end up paying an emotional fortune. You may never be the same again.
- If you do not guard your heart, you could meet a man that will destroy the core essence of who you were created to be; your personality, compassion, generosity etc.

A SELAH MOMENT:

Who sent this man to you? Are you using patience to help bring clarity and assurance that this man is heaven sent and not hell sent? Are your eyes truly open to see what is really going on in this relationship? Don't rush the process, God will speak!

_____

_____

_____

CHAPTER TWENTY ONE

Where Is Boaz

In order to be found, you have to be seen!

To my sisters who are re-entering the dating scene after many, many years of sacrificing your lives for children and ex-husbands, or perhaps you locked yourself away due to some traumatic pain. Maybe you've given yourself to working in the ministry, thinking your Boaz is gonna come, only to find out that the brook done dried up and ain't no water comin'. Therefore, like Elijah, you've got to move from that place and do something different. Dating and how we meet men have drastically changed.

If you want a Boaz, you got to GET UP, GET OUT, and GO to Boaz field. You've got to go to where Boaz is so that you can be seen and found by him. It seems like there are no good men who are husband material left, but they are out there, you just got to go to where they are. If Ruth had not gone to Boaz field; the place where Boaz hung out, the place where he lived, Boaz would have never seen and found her. In order to be found, you have to be seen.

For those of you who are not familiar with the story of Boaz and Ruth, I will provide a brief summary:

A Hebrew woman by the name of Naomi, along with her husband and two sons went to live in a foreign country due to a severe famine in Bethlehem. The two sons married women from a foreign land, one of them was named Ruth. Eventually Naomi's husband, and two sons died. Therefore, Naomi decided to return back to Bethlehem and encouraged her two daughter-in-laws to return back to their families. However, Ruth decided to follow Naomi back to her country.

In order to obtain food, Naomi encouraged Ruth to go and glean grain from the field of her wealthy kinsman Boaz. As Ruth was working, Boaz was observing and checking her out. Boaz inquired about Ruth: he liked what he heard and saw. He told Ruth not to go and glean in anyone else's field. Boaz started leaving extra grain for her. Naomi realized what was happening, and coached Ruth, to put on her best clothes and perfume and visit Boaz during the night time. Boaz ended up drinking a bit, fell asleep and when he awakened, he found Ruth laying at his feet. From that night on, Boaz wanted to marry Ruth and he eventually did.

Sisters of the Faith have been told, stop focusing so much on trying to get a husband. God knows your address, **BE PATIENT** and when God is ready, He will send him to you. The man will find you. The Word says, **he** that finds, not **she** that finds. You just keep on doing what you are doing, focusing on God and he will come.

It's been more than ten years now and still no Boaz. You look around in your church and the churches that you visit; and see little to no men. And, the ones who are there, you don't want. The good ones in the church seem to all be taken. So you keep waiting and waiting and waiting.

Honey child, Boaz may or may not be in the church house. You may be found by him on a dating site. You may be found by him on the golf course. You may be found by him at a sporting event. You may be found by him at a car show etc. Increase your chances of meeting a man by going to places where you can be seen by them. GO TO THE PLACES WHERE MEN HANG OUT. Stop limiting God, saying He's only going to move in one particular way.

Now that being said, let's talk about the word *patience* and the word *wait*. When God tells us to be patient and wait, does that mean that we do nothing about our situation? No, I believe God is saying **be patient but proactive.** Let's examine the word *proactive*. One definition of the word *proactive* means "to cause to happen." In other words, you are praying and you are **taking action** and putting yourself in a position to be found. Think about it this way, if you pray and ask God for a job, you get busy researching openings, putting in resumes and applications. You want to buy a house, you get busy saving, getting your credit straight, contacting a realtor and looking at homes. In every area of our lives we are actively causing a desired result to come to pass. You just don't pray and that's it. Approximately thirty years ago, we could pray and do nothing else to meet someone, but for the most part not today.

Now, let's examine the word *wait*. I believe that the word *wait*, when it comes to dating, means that once you meet someone, you WAIT and let God reveal to you whether or not this person is the right one for you. Too often women of the faith want to make a husband out of the first man that comes along. Pump your brakes, gather the facts, and put your emotions on hold. However, you might have to kiss a few frogs before your prince charming comes along.

Girls, be patient and work the process and don't give up. He may not be as tall as you like, so what, as long as he treats you right. He may not be the race that you like, so what, as long as he treats you right. He may be a little older than you like, so what, as long as he treats you right. He may not be as articulate as you like. So what? As long as he treats you right. I think you get the point.

Boaz is out there! Be patient with the process, and don't give up! I am praying that you have much success being found by your Boaz. Love y'all.

ABOUT THE AUTHOR

Tammy Calderon is a woman of many talents. She is a Christian counselor, singer, songwriter, author, and entrepreneur. She graduated from the University of California at Los Angeles (UCLA) and resides in the Dallas area where she loves to spend time with family and friends. Tammy comes from a large family, she is the seventh of nine children and grew up in a small town in East Texas called Naples, a country girl of sorts.

She has always had a heart for troubled youth; therefore, most of her career life was dedicated to working with and mentoring "youth at risk."

One of Tammy's passions is to see the survival of strong marriages and families. Over the last several years, it seems as though people have become quite cynical about love and marriage. Many are beginning to shy away from one of our oldest institutions. Through her writings, Tammy's desire is to rekindle the hope that it is still possible to find that special someone in whom you can build a relationship that is healthy, satisfying, lasting, and strong.

CPSIA information can be obtained
at www.ICGtesting.com
Printed in the USA
LVHW010341060820
662303LV00004B/460